**IMPACTING EARTH**
HOW PEOPLE CHANGE THE LAND

MAKING DAMS AND RESERVOIRS

ELIZABETH KRAJNIK

PowerKiDS press
New York

Published in 2019 by The Rosen Publishing Group, Inc.
29 East 21st Street, New York, NY 10010

Copyright © 2019 by The Rosen Publishing Group, Inc.

All rights reserved. No part of this book may be reproduced in any form without permission in writing from the publisher, except by a reviewer.

First Edition

Editor: Jennifer Lombardo
Book Design: Tanya Dellaccio

Photo Credits: Cover superjoseph/Shutterstock.com; p. 4 Mavermick/Shutterstock.com; p. 5 turtix/Shutterstock.com; p. 7 kwanchai.c/Shutterstock.com; p. 9 JENNY VAUGHAN/AFP/Getty Images; p. 11 Gary Saxe/Shutterstock/com; pp. 12, 13 JOSH EDELSON/AFP/Getty Images; p. 15 (inset) Johnny Habell/Shutterstock.com; p. 15 (main) Kletr/Shutterstock.com; p. 17 Olga Kashubin/Shutterstock.com; p. 19 Akatjomar/Shutterstock.com; p. 21 Richard Whitcombe/Shutterstock.com; p. 22 Juan Enrique del Barrio/Shutterstock.com.

Library of Congress Cataloging-in-Publication Data

Names: Krajnik, Elizabeth, author.
Title: Making dams and reservoirs / Elizabeth Krajnik.
Description: New York : PowerKids Press, [2019] | Series: Impacting Earth: how people change the land | Includes index.
Identifiers: LCCN 2018028494| ISBN 9781538341940 (library bound) | ISBN 9781538341926 (pbk.) | ISBN 9781538341933 (6 pack)
Subjects: LCSH: Dams–Juvenile literature. | Dams–Design and construction–Juvenile literature. | Reservoirs–Juvenile literature. | Hydrology–Juvenile literature. | Nature–Effect of human beings on–Juvenile literature.
Classification: LCC TC541 .K73 2019 | DDC 627/.8–dc23
LC record available at https://lccn.loc.gov/2018028494

Manufactured in the United States of America

CPSIA Compliance Information: Batch #CWPK19. For Further Information contact Rosen Publishing, New York, New York at 1-800-237-9932

CONTENTS

IMPORTANT STRUCTURES 4
PARTS OF A DAM 6
HOW ARE DAMS BUILT? 8
WHY ARE DAMS IMPORTANT? 10
NEGATIVE EFFECTS OF DAMS 12
KINDS OF RESERVOIRS 14
HOW ARE RESERVOIRS BUILT? 16
WHY ARE RESERVOIRS
   IMPORTANT? 18
NEGATIVE EFFECTS
   OF RESERVOIRS 20
CHANGING THE LAND
   FOR THE BETTER 22
GLOSSARY 23
INDEX 24
WEBSITES 24

IMPORTANT STRUCTURES

A dam is a natural or man-made **structure** built across a stream or river to hold back water. A reservoir is a natural or man-made structure where water is gathered for humans to use. These structures are very important to human life today. Without them, many people wouldn't have water.

RESERVOIR

PARTS OF A DAM

Many dams look a little like a human foot from the side. On the side where the water flows, or moves, toward the dam, there is a "heel." On the downstream side, where the water flows away from the dam, there is a "toe." Dams also have a spillway, which is a structure through or over which floodwaters can safely be directed downstream.

KEEPING WATCH
Near the heel, there's a window through which workers can check to make sure the dam is working.

HOW ARE DAMS BUILT?

To build most dams, **engineers** must take water out of the river that's being dammed. They do this by building a tunnel that goes around where the dam will be built. The river's water will run through this tunnel. Then workers can begin removing rocks and building the dam. All of this work can have a large effect on the land.

WHY ARE DAMS IMPORTANT?

Dams are important for many reasons. Some dams make **electricity**, which people use to power their homes and businesses. Dams also make it possible for people to store water. Farmers use this water for their plants. Other people use stored water in their homes or businesses. In some places, dams keep rivers from flooding during rainy periods.

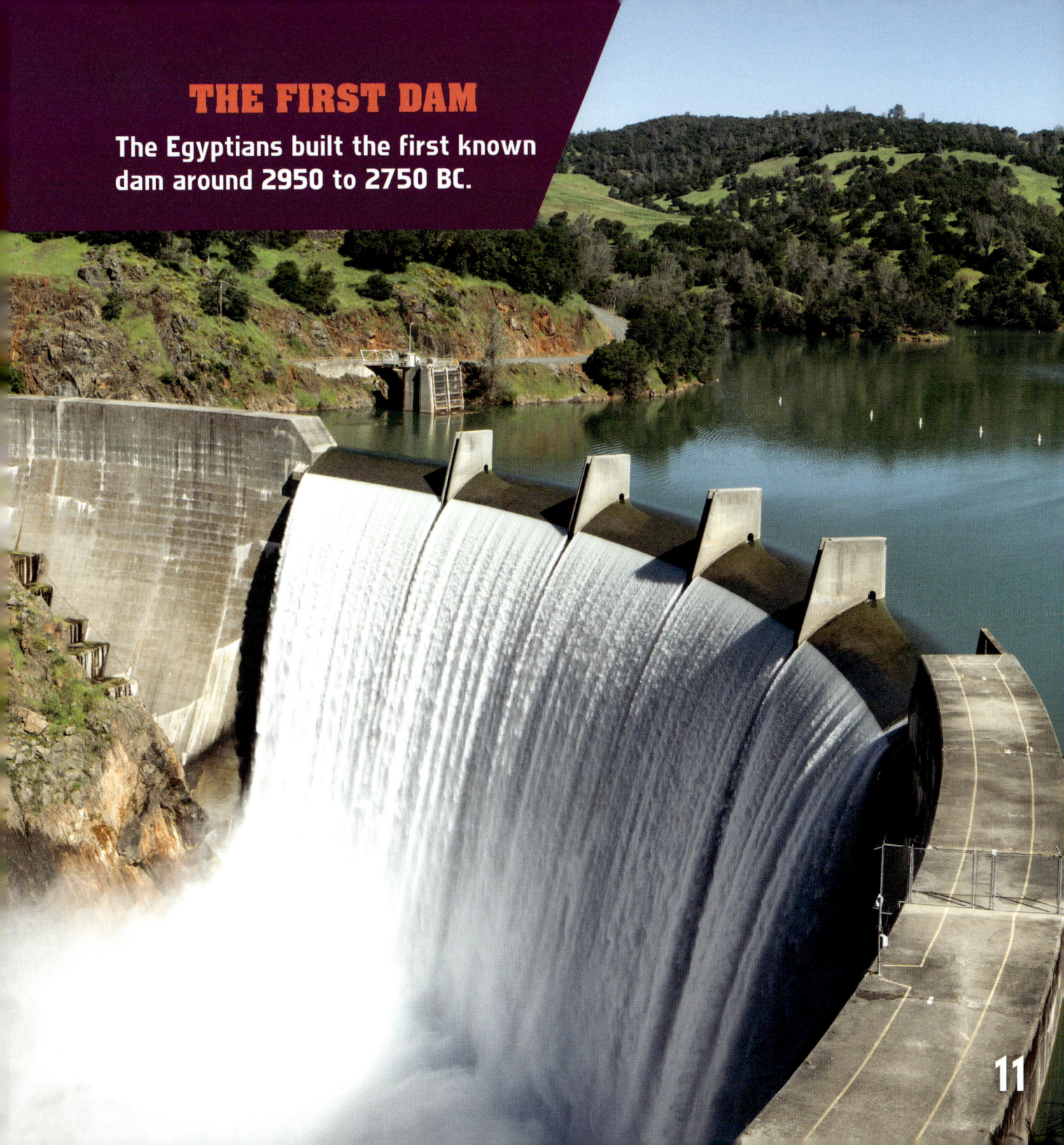

THE FIRST DAM
The Egyptians built the first known dam around 2950 to 2750 BC.

NEGATIVE EFFECTS OF DAMS

Even though dams are good for most humans, they can change the land in negative, or bad, ways. When people build a dam, the water has to go somewhere. Engineers change where the waters flow. This may mean that people or animals can't continue living there because the land will flood. In other areas, people may not get the water they need to survive.

REMOVING DAMS

More than 1,000 dams have been removed in the United States because they didn't create enough electricity or they caused negative **effects**.

KINDS OF RESERVOIRS

Some reservoirs are formed by damming the **outlet** of a natural lake, which controls how much water flows out of the lake. However, some reservoirs are built away from dams. These fully man-made reservoirs are called service reservoirs or cisterns. A water tower is an example of a cistern. Some reservoirs change an area that used to be land to one covered with water.

CISTERN

15

HOW ARE RESERVOIRS BUILT?

Dams are the most common way to make reservoirs. The upstream area floods and becomes a storage space for water. In the case of cisterns, engineers may build towers into which water is **pumped**. They may also remove trees and other plants from the land, dig a large hole, and fill it with water.

WHY ARE RESERVOIRS IMPORTANT?

Humans need reservoirs for several reasons. We use reservoirs to water crops. They hold the water that comes from melting mountain snow so it doesn't flood towns near the mountains. They also give people water during droughts, which are periods of time when it doesn't rain much. Droughts may make it hard to find water in places other than reservoirs. We also use reservoirs for boating, swimming, and other activities.

GIVING US FRESH WATER
Reservoirs are an important source of fresh water.

NEGATIVE EFFECTS OF RESERVOIRS

The water in reservoirs doesn't move much. Because it stays so still, **sediment** in the water ends up on the bottom of the reservoir. Over time, the reservoir will fill up with sediment and have less room to hold water. Water in reservoirs also evaporates very quickly. This means it turns to a gas called water vapor. These things can make reservoirs less useful.

21

CHANGING THE LAND FOR THE BETTER

Even though there are negative effects of dams and reservoirs, these structures are very important to human life. Without them, many people wouldn't be able to water their crops and others would suffer from the effects of flooding. We must be careful when planning these structures so we don't change the land in ways that hurt people, animals, and plants.

GLOSSARY

effect: Something that happens as a result of something else.

electricity: A form of energy that is carried through wires and is used to operate machines, lights, etc.

engineer: Someone who plans and builds machines.

outlet: A place or opening for letting something out.

pump: To move a gas or liquid from one place to another.

sediment: Matter, such as rocks, sand, and stones, that is moved and deposited by water, wind, or glaciers.

structure: A building or other object that is built.

INDEX

A
Australia, 17

C
cistern, 14, 15, 16

D
drought, 18

E
Egyptians, 11
electricity, 10, 13
engineer, 8, 12, 16

H
heel, 6, 7
Hoover Dam, 5

L
lake, 14

R
river, 4, 8, 10

S
sediment, 20
service reservoir, 14
spillway, 6
stream, 4

T
toe, 6
tunnel, 8

U
United States, 13

W
water, 4, 6, 8, 10, 12, 14, 16, 18, 19, 20
water tower, 14, 16

WEBSITES

Due to the changing nature of Internet links, PowerKids Press has developed an online list of websites related to the subject of this book. This site is updated regularly. Please use this link to access the list: www.powerkidslinks.com/hpcl/dams